# JAZZ
# STANDARDS

**MELODY LINE, CHORDS AND LYRICS**
**FOR KEYBOARD • GUITAR • VOCAL**

ISBN 0-7935-8872-3

HAL•LEONARD®
CORPORATION
7777 W. BLUEMOUND RD. P.O. BOX 13819 MILWAUKEE, WI 53213

Visit Hal Leonard Online at
**www.halleonard.com**

Welcome to the PAPERBACK SONGS SERIES

Do you play piano, guitar, electronic keyboard, sing or play any instrument for that matter? If so, this handy "pocket tune" book is for you.

The concise, one-line music notation consists of:

## MELODY, LYRICS & CHORD SYMBOLS

Whether strumming the chords on guitar, "faking" an arrangement on piano/keyboard or singing the lyrics, these fake book style arrangements can be enjoyed at any experience level – hobbyist to professional.

The musical skills necessary to successfully use this book are minimal. If you play guitar and need some help with chords, a basic chord chart is included at the back of the book.

While playing and singing is the first thing that comes to mind when using this book, it can also serve as a compact, comprehensive reference guide.

However you choose to use this PAPERBACK SONGS SERIES book, by all means have fun!

# CONTENTS

*(contents continued)*

# ALFIE
### Theme from the Paramount Picture ALFIE

Words by HAL DAVID
Music by BURT BACHARACH

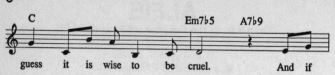

guess it is wise to be cruel. And if

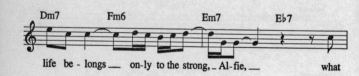

life be-longs __ on-ly to the strong, __ Al-fie, __ what

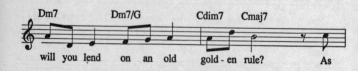

will you lend on an old gold-en rule? As

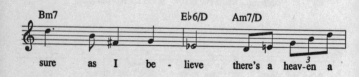

sure as I be - lieve there's a heav-en a

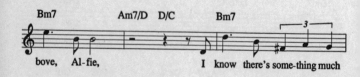

bove, Al-fie, I know there's some-thing much

more, some-thing e - ven non - be-liev - ers

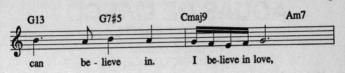

can    be - lieve    in.    I  be-lieve in love,

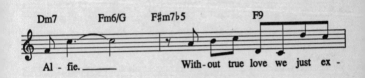

Al - fie. _____    With - out true love we just ex -

ist,    Al - fie.    Un - til you find the love you've

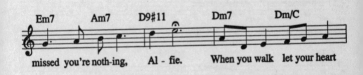

missed you're noth-ing,    Al - fie.    When you walk  let your heart

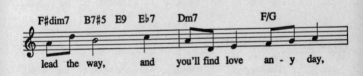

lead  the  way,    and    you'll find love    an - y  day,

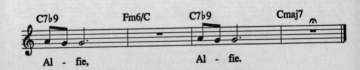

Al - fie,    Al - fie.

# AGUAS DE MARCO
## (WATERS OF MARCH)

Words and Music by
ANTONIO CARLOS JOBIM

A stick, a stone, it's the end of the road. __ It's the rest of a stump, __ it's a lit-tle a-lone. __ It's a sli-ver of glass, __ it is life, __ it's the sun, __ it is night, __ it is death, __ it's a trap, __ it's a gun. __ The oak when it blooms, __ a fox in the brush, __ the knot in the wood, __ the song of a thrush, __ the wood of the wind, __ a cliff, a fall, __ a scratch, a lump, __

it is noth - ing at all. ___ It's the wind blow-ing free, ___

___ it's the end ___ of the slope, ___ it's a beam, it's a void, ___

___ it's a hunch, ___ it's a hope, ___ And the riv - er - bank

talks of the Wa-ters Of March. ___ It's the end of the strain, ___

___ it's the joy ___ in your heart. ___ The foot, the

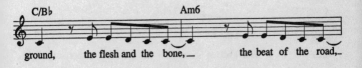

ground, the flesh and the bone, ___ the beat of the road, ___

___ a sling - shot stone, ___ a fish, a flash, ___

and the riv-er-bank talks of the Wa-ters Of March.

It's the prom-ise of life, in your heart, in your heart.

A stick, a stone, the end of the load,

the rest of a stump, a lone-some road,

a sli-ver of glass, a life, the sun,

a night, a death, the end of the run,

and the riv-er-bank talks of the Wa-ters Of March.

It's the end of all strain, it's the joy in your heart.

# ALL THE THINGS YOU ARE

**from VERY WARM FOR MAY**

Lyrics by OSCAR HAMMERSTEIN II
Music by JEROME KERN

Moderately

You are the prom-ised kiss of spring-time That makes the lone-ly win-ter seem long. _____ You are the breath-less hush of eve-ning That trem-bles on the brink of a love-ly song. _____ You are the

an - gel glow ____ that lights a star. ____

____ The dear - est things I know ____

____ are what you are.

Some day my hap - py arms will

hold you, And some day I'll

know that mo - ment di - vine. When All The Things You

Are, are mine. ____

# <sup>18</sup>ALRIGHT, OKAY, YOU WIN

### Words and Music by SID WYCHE and MAYME WATTS

# APRIL IN PARIS

Words by E.Y. HARBURG
Music by VERNON DUKE

# AUTUMN IN NEW YORK

Words and Music by
VERNON DUKE

**Slowly**

Gm7 | Am7 | B♭maj7 | C7

Au-tumn In New York, _____ why does it seem so in-

Fmaj7 | Am7 | D7 | Gm7 | Am7

vit - ing? _____ Au-tumn In New York, _____

B♭maj7 | C7 | Am7♭5 | D7

_____ it spells the thrill of first night - ing. _____

Gm7 | B♭m7 | E♭7

Glit - ter - ing crowds and shim-mer - ing clouds in

A♭maj7 | G7 | Cm7

can - yons of steel, _____ they're mak-ing me feel _____

G7 | Cmaj7 | Am7 | D7

_____ I'm home. _____ It's

# BEWITCHED
## from PAL JOEY

Words by LORENZ HART
Music by RICHARD RODGERS

# BILL
## from SHOW BOAT

**Lyrics by P.G. WODEHOUSE and OSCAR HAMMERSTEIN II**
**Music by JEROME KERN**

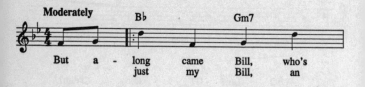

Moderately — B♭ — Gm7

But a - long came Bill, who's
just my Bill, an

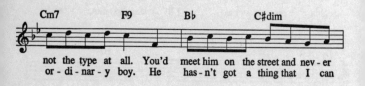

Cm7 — F9 — B♭ — C#dim

not the type at all. You'd meet him on the street and nev - er
or - di - nar - y boy. He has - n't got a thing that I can

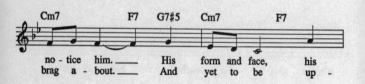

Cm7 — F7 — G7♯5 — Cm7 — F7

no - tice him. ___ His form and face, his
brag a - bout. ___ And yet to be up -

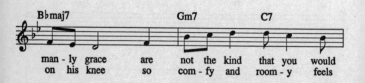

B♭maj7 — Gm7 — C7

man - ly grace are not the kind that you would
on his knee so com - fy and room - y would feels

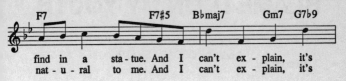

find in a sta - tue. And I can't ex - plain, it's
nat - u - ral to me. And I can't ex - plain, it's

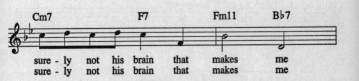

sure - ly not his brain that makes me
sure - ly not his brain that makes me

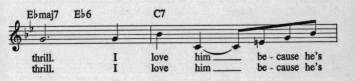

thrill. I love him ____ be - cause he's
thrill. I love him ____ be - cause he's

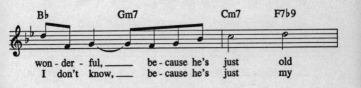

won - der - ful, ____ be - cause he's just old
I don't know, ____ be - cause he's just my

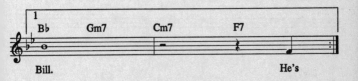

Bill. He's

Bill. ____

# BLAME IT ON MY YOUTH

Words by EDWARD HEYMAN
Music by OSCAR LEVANT

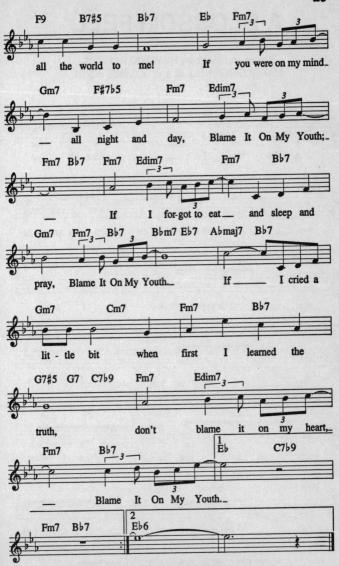

# A BLOSSOM FELL

**Words and Music by HOWARD BARNES,
HAROLD CORNELIUS and DOMINIC JOHN**

Slow Ballad | Bb6 | Bdim7

A Blos - som Fell＿＿＿ from off a

Cm7 | F7 | F7#5

tree,＿＿＿ it set - tled soft - ly on the lips you turned to

Bb | Bbmaj7/D | C#dim7

me.＿＿＿ The gyp - sies say, and I know

Cm7 | F7 | Cm7 | F7 | F7#5

why,＿＿＿ a fall - ing blos - som on - ly

Bb | Bdim7 | Cm7 | F7

touch - es lips that lie. A Blos - som

Bb6 | Bdim7 | Cm7

Fell,＿＿＿ and ver - y soon＿＿＿ I saw you

31

# BLUESETTE

Words by NORMAN GIMBEL
Music by JEAN THIELEMANS

Bm7　　Bb7　　Am7　　D7

way.
stay.

G　　F#m7b5　　B7

Get set, Blues-ette,　　true love is com-ing.

Em7　　A7　　Dm7　　G7

Your trou-bled heart　　soon will be hum-ming.

Cmaj7　　C6　　Cm7　　F7

*Hum.*

Bbmaj7　　Bb6　　Bbm7　　Eb9

Abmaj7　　Am7b5　　D7b9

Doo-ya, doo-ya, doo-ya, doo-ya, doo-ya, doo-ya, Doo-oo-oo Blues-

Bm7　　Bb7　　Am7　　D7

ette.

Pret-ty lit-tle Blues-ette    must-n't be a mourn-er.

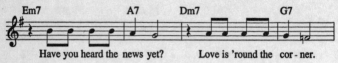

Have you heard the news yet?    Love is 'round the cor-ner.

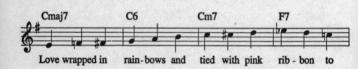

Love wrapped in    rain-bows and    tied with pink    rib-bon to

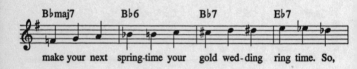

make your next    spring-time your    gold wed-ding    ring time. So,

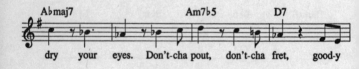

dry    your    eyes. Don't-cha pout,    don't-cha fret,    good-y

good times    are    com-ing,    Blues-ette. _____

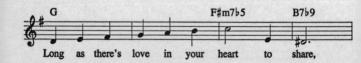

Long    as    there's    love    in    your    heart    to    share,

# BYE BYE BLACKBIRD

**from PETE KELLY'S BLUES**

Lyric by MORT DIXON
Music by RAY HENDERSON

38

# CALL ME IRRESPONSIBLE
## from the Paramount Picture PAPA'S DELICATE CONDITION

Words by SAMMY CAHN
Music by JAMES VAN HEUSEN

**Slowly**

Call Me Ir - re - spon - si - ble, call me

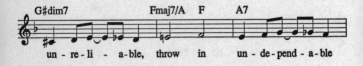

un - re - li - a - ble, throw in un - de - pend - a - ble

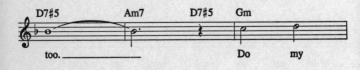

too. _____ Do my

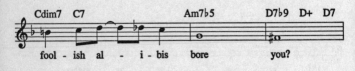

fool - ish al - i - bis bore you?

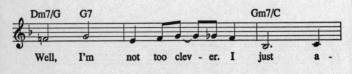

Well, I'm not too clev - er. I just a -

dore you. Call me un - pre - dict - a - ble,

tell me I'm im‑prac‑ti‑cal, rain‑bows

I'm in‑clined to pur‑sue. ___

Call Me Ir‑re‑spon‑si‑ble, yes, I'm

un‑re‑li‑a‑ble, but it's

un‑de‑ni‑a‑bly true, ___ I'm

ir‑re‑spon‑si‑bly mad for you! ___

___ you! ___

# CAN'T HELP LOVIN' DAT MAN

**from SHOW BOAT**

Lyrics by OSCAR HAMMERSTEIN II
Music by JEROME KERN

| Gm7 | C7♭9 | F6 | | F#dim7 |

When he goes a - way ___

| Cmaj7 | | D7 | Em7 | E♭maj7 |

dat's a rain - y day, ___ and when he comes

| Dm7 | D9 | Dm7/G | | G7 |

back dat day is fine, ___ the sun will shine.

| Cmaj7 | Am7 | Dm7 | | G7 |

He can come home ___ as late as can be, ___

| Cmaj7 | Gm7 | C7♭9 | F6 | B♭9 |

home with - out him ___ ain't no home to me, ___

| Em7 | Am7 | A♭7 | D7♭9 | G7♭9 |

Can't Help Lov-in' Dat Man ___ of

| Cmaj7 | E♭9 | A♭maj7 | D♭maj7 | Cmaj7 |

mine. _____

# CARAVAN

## from SOPHISTICATED LADIES

**Words and Music by DUKE ELLINGTON,
IRVING MILLS and JUAN TIZOL**

on our Car - a - van. _____
of our Car - a - van. _____
des - sert Car - a - van. _____

**Fine**

This _____ is so ex - cit -

ing, you _____ are so in -

vit - ing rest - ing in my

arms as I thrill to _____

_____ the mag - ic charms _____ of

**D.C. al Fine**

# C'EST SI BON
## (It's So Good)

English Words by JERRY SEELEN
French Words by ANDRE HORNEZ
Music by HENRI BETTI

**Moderately**

"C'est Si Bon," _____ lov - ers say that in
Bon," _____ De par - tir n'im porte
Bon," _____ De pou voir l'em bras -

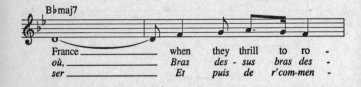

France _____ when they thrill to ro -
où, _____ Bras des - sus bras des -
ser _____ Et puis de r'com - men -

mance, _____ it means that it's so good..
sous _____ En chan - tant des chan - sons. _
cer _____ A la moindre oc - ca - sion. _

_____ C'est Si Bon,
_____ C'est Si Bon, _____
_____ C'est Si Bon, _____

46

good, _____ noth - ing else can re -
*Bon,* _____ *De guet - ter dans ses*
*Bon,* _____ *Quand j'la tiens dans mes*

place, _____ just your slight - est em - brace. _____
*yeux,* _____ *Un es - poir mer - veil leux* _____
*bras.* _____ *De me dir' - que tout ca* _____

___ And if you on - ly would, _____ be my
___ *Qui don - ne le fris - son.* _____ *C'est Si*
___ *C'est á moi pour de bon.* _____ *C'est Si*

own, _____ for the rest of my
*Bon,* _____ *Ces pe - tit's sen - sa*
*Bon,* _____ *Et si nous nous ai -*

days. _____ I will whis - per this
*tions.* _____ *Ça vaut moiux qu'un mil -*
*mons.* _____ *Cher - chez pas la rai -*

phrase, _____ my dar - ling, "C'est Si Bon."
*lion.* _____ *Tell' - ment, tell' - ment c'est bon.* _____
*son* _____ *C'est parc' que C'est Si Bon.* _____

**1** Bb      Cm7      F7      N.C.

"C'est      Si
"C'est      *Si*
"C'est      *Si*

**2** Bb    Gm7    Cm7      F7

I mean   that it's   so      good,_

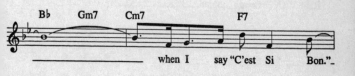

Bb    Gm7    Cm7      F7

when I    say "C'est Si    Bon."_

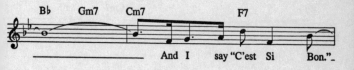

Bb    Gm7    Cm7      F7

And I    say "C'est Si    Bon."_

Bb    Gm7    Cm7      F7

Be-cause   it's oh,   so      good._

Bb6

# COME RAIN
# OR COME SHINE
### from ST. LOUIS WOMAN

**Words by JOHNNY MERCER**
**Music by HAROLD ARLEN**

# CRY ME A RIVER

### Words and Music by
### ARTHUR HAMILTON

You drove me,— near-ly drove me out of my head,— while

you ____ nev-er shed a tear. ____

Re-mem-ber?— I re-mem-ber all that you said;—

told me love was too ple-be-ian, told me you were thru with me, an'

Now ____ you say you love me, ____

well, just to prove you do, ____ come on, an'

Cry ____ Me A Riv-er, Cry__ Me A Riv-er,

I cried a riv-er o-ver you.____ you.

# DEARLY BELOVED

**from YOU WERE NEVER LOVELIER**

Music by JEROME KERN
Words by JOHNNY MERCER

**Moderately**

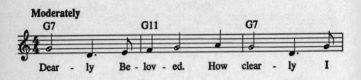

Dear - ly Be - lov - ed. How clear - ly I

see. Some - where in heav - en you were

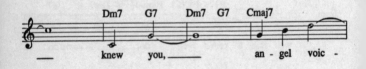

fash - ioned for me. An - gels eyes _____

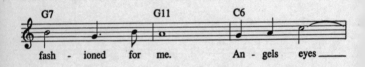

_____ knew you, _____ an - gel voic -

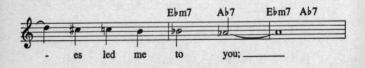

- es led me to you; _____

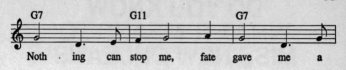

Noth - ing can stop me, fate gave me a

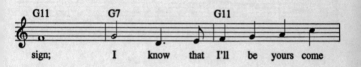

sign; I know that I'll be yours come

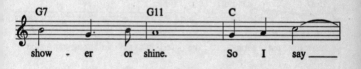

show - er or shine. So I say ____

____ mere - ly. ____ Dear - ly Be -

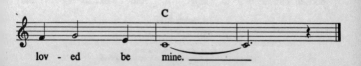

lov - ed be mine. ____

# DO YOU KNOW WHAT IT MEANS TO MISS NEW ORLEANS

Lyric by EDDIE DE LANGE
Music by LOUIS ALTER

# DON'T EXPLAIN

Words and Music by BILLIE HOLIDAY
and ARTHUR HERZOG

**Slowly**

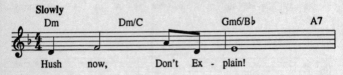

Hush now, Don't Ex - plain!

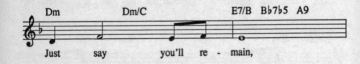

Just say you'll re - main,

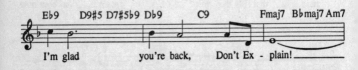

I'm glad you're back, Don't Ex - plain! _____

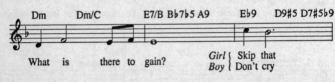

_____ Qui - et, Don't Ex - plain!

What is there to gain? *Girl* { Skip that
*Boy* { Don't cry

lip - stick, }
don't lie; } Don't Ex - plain! _____

57

# DON'T GET AROUND MUCH ANYMORE

Words and Music by BOB RUSSELL
and DUKE ELLINGTON

Medium swing

Missed the Sat-ur-day dance, heard they crowd-ed the floor; could-n't bear it with-out you, Don't Get A-round Much An-y-more.

Thought I'd vis-it the club, got as far as the door; they'd have asked me a-bout you, Don't Get A-round Much An-y-more.

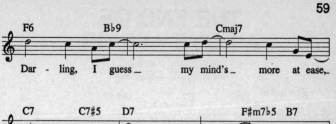

Dar - ling, I guess _ my mind's _ more at ease, _

_ but nev - er - the - less _

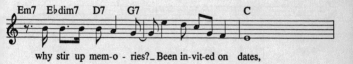

why stir up mem-o - ries? _ Been in-vit-ed on dates,

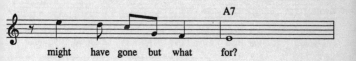

might have gone but what for?

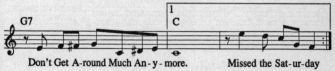

Aw - f'lly dif - f'rent with - out _ you, _

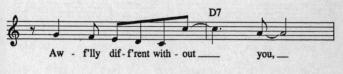

Don't Get A-round Much An - y - more.     Missed the Sat - ur - day

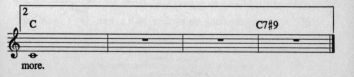

more.

# THE END OF A LOVE AFFAIR

Words and Music by
EDWARD C. REDDING

# EV'RY TIME
# WE SAY GOODBYE
### from SEVEN LIVELY ARTS

**Words and Music by**
**COLE PORTER**

# FINE AND MELLOW

### Words and Music by
### BILLIE HOLIDAY

**Moderately slow Blues**

My man don't love me, treats me oh so mean, _____ my man he don't love _ me, treats me aw - ful mean, _____ he's the low - est man that I've ev - er seen. He wears high-draped pants, _

stripes are real-ly yel-low; _____ he wears

high-draped pants, ___ stripes are real-ly yel-

low. But when he

starts in to love me he's so Fine And

Mel-low. _____ Love will

make you drink and gam-ble, make you stay out all night

long. _____ Love will

# A FINE ROMANCE
## from SWING TIME

Words by DOROTHY FIELDS
Music by JEROME KERN

# THE FOLKS WHO LIVE ON THE HILL

**from HIGH, WIDE AND HANDSOME**
Lyrics by OSCAR HAMMERSTEIN II
Music by JEROME KERN

Some - day _____ we'll build a home on a a
Some - day _____ we may be add - ing a

hill - top high, _____ you and I. _____
thing or two, _____ a wing or two, _____

Shin - y and new, _____ a cot - tage that two _____ can
we will make change - es as an - y fam - 'ly

fill. _____ And we'll be pleased to be called_
will. _____ But we will al - ways be called_

_____ "The Folks Who Live On The Hill." _____
_____ "The Folks Who Live On The Hill." _____

Our _____ ve - ran - da

F#m7b5     B7     Em     Em#7

will com-mand a view of mead-ows green, _____ the sort of

Em7     A9b5     D7     G     G7

view that seems to want to be seen. _____

Dm7     G7#5     Cmaj7     C7

__ And when the kids grow up and leave us, _____

Fmaj7     G11     C/E     Ebdim7     Dm6     Am/C

__ we'll sit and look at that same old view,__ just we two.__

Em7     Am7     Dm7     G7#5

Dar-by and Joan,__ who used to be Jack__ and

Cmaj7     C7     Fmaj7     G7

Jill, _____ the folks who like to be called__

Em     A7b9     Dm7     G7

_____ what they have al-ways been called,__

E     A7     D7     G7

_____ "The Folks Who Live On The Hill."__

C     C7     Fm7     C

# FRENESI

### Words and Music by
### ALBERTO DOMINGUEZ

# GEORGIA ON MY MIND

Words by STUART GORRELL
Music by HOAGY CARMICHAEL

77

# THE GIRL FROM IPANEMA
## (Garôta de Ipanema)

English Words by NORMAN GIMBEL
Original Words by VINICIUS DE MORAES
Music by ANTONIO CARLOS JOBIM

# GIRL TALK
### from the Paramount Picture HARLOW

Words by BOBBY TROUP
Music by NEAL HEFTI

**Slowly and bluesy**

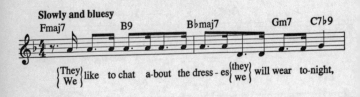

{They/We} like to chat a-bout the dress-es {they/we} will wear to-night,

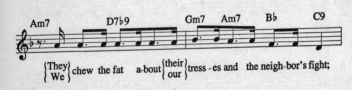

{They/We} chew the fat a-bout {their/our} tress-es and the neigh-bor's fight;

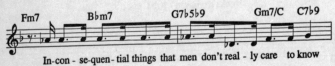

In-con-se-quen-tial things that men don't real-ly care to know

be-come es-sen-tial things that wom-en find so "ap-pro-po."

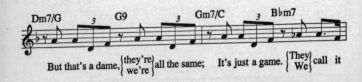

But that's a dame, {they're/we're} all the same; It's just a game. {They/We} call it

# THE GLORY OF LOVE

### from GUESS WHO'S COMING TO DINNER

Words and Music by
BILLY HILL

**Medium beat**

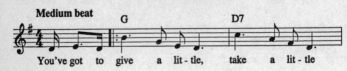

You've got to give a lit-tle, take a lit-tle

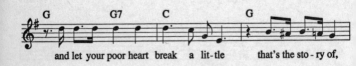

and let your poor heart break a lit-tle that's the sto-ry of,

that's The Glo-ry Of Love._____ You've got to

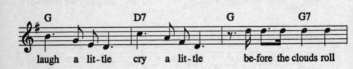

laugh a lit-tle cry a lit-tle be-fore the clouds roll

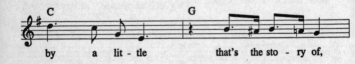

by a lit-tle that's the sto-ry of,

that's The Glo-ry Of Love._____ As

long as there's the two of us we've got the world and all its charms. And when the world is through with us we've got each oth-er's arms. You've got to win a lit-tle, lose a lit-tle and al-ways have the blues a lit-tle. That's the sto-ry of, that's The Glo-ry Of Love.

You've got to Love.

# GOOD MORNING HEARTACHE

**Words and Music by DAN FISHER,
IRENE HIGGINBOTHAM and ERVIN DRAKE**

# GOD BLESS' THE CHILD

### Words and Music by ARTHUR HERZOG JR.
### and BILLIE HOLIDAY

Slowly, with feeling

Them that's got shall get, them that's not shall lose, so the
strong gets more, while the weak ones fade, emp-ty

Bi - ble said, and it still is news; }
pock - ets don't ev - er make the grade, }

Ma - ma may have, Pa - pa may have, but

God Bless' The Child that's got his own! That's

got his own. Yes, the

# GREEN EYES
## (AQUELLOS OJOS VERDES)

**Words and Music by ADOLFO UTRERA
and NILO MENDEZ**

Your Green Eyes with their soft lights,___ your eyes that prom-ise

sweet nights ___ bring to my soul a long - ing ___

___ a thirst for love di - vine.___ In dreams I seem to

hold you ___ to find you and en -

fold you ___ our lips meet, and our

hearts too, ___ with a thrill so sub -

lime. ___ Those cool and lim - pid

# HARLEM NOCTURNE

Words by DICK ROGERS
Music by EARLE HAGEN

Deep mu-sic fills the night,_____ deep in the heart of Har-
_____ a noc-turne born in Har-

-lem._____ And tho' the stars are bright,_____
-lem._____ That mel-an-cho-ly strain _____

_____ the dark-ness is taun-ting me.
_____ for-ev-er is haunt-ing me.

Oh, what a sad re-frain,_____ The

mel-o-dy clings ___ a-round my heart strings. ___ It
in-di-go tune ___ it sings to the moon ___ the

won't let me go ___ when I'm lone-ly, ___ I
lone-some re-frain ___ of a lov-er. ___ The

hear it in dreams __ and some-how it seems __ it
mel - o - dy sighs, __ it laughs and it cries, __ a

makes __ me __ weep __ and __ I __ can't __ sleep. An
moan __ in __ blue __ that __

wails __ the __ long __ night __ thru. __

__ Tho' with the dawn it's gone, __ the mel-o-dy lives ev -

- er __ for lone-ly hearts to learn __

__ of love in a Har-lem Noc-turne. __

# HOW ABOUT ME?

Words and Music by
IRVING BERLIN

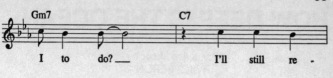

I to do? \_\_\_ I'll still re -

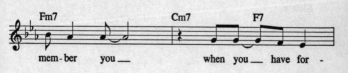

mem - ber you \_\_\_ when you \_\_\_ have for -

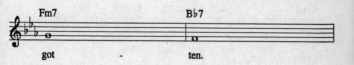

got - ten.

And may - be a ba - by

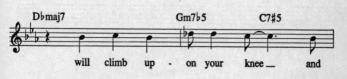

will climb up - on your knee \_\_\_ and

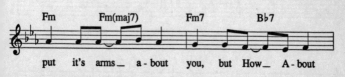

put it's arms \_\_\_ a - bout you, but How \_\_\_ A - bout

Me? _____

# HOW DEEP IS THE OCEAN
## (HOW HIGH IS THE SKY)

Words and Music by
IRVING BERLIN

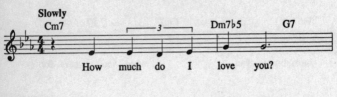

How much do I love you?

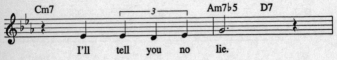

I'll tell you no lie.

How Deep Is The O - cean,

how high is the sky?

How man - y times a day __ do

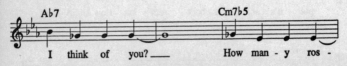

I think of you? __ How man - y ros -

# HOW HIGH THE MOON

**from TWO FOR THE SHOW**

Words by NANCY HAMILTON
Music by MORGAN LEWIS

# HOW INSENSITIVE
## (INSENSATEZ)

Original Words by VINICIUS DE MORAES
English Words by NORMAN GIMBEL
Music by ANTONIO CARLOS JOBIM

# I CAN'T GET
# STARTED WITH YOU

**from ZIEGFELD FOLLIES**

Words by IRA GERSHWIN
Music by VERNON DUKE

I've flown a-round the world in a plane; ___ I've set-tled
hun-dred yards in ten flat; _____ the Prince of

re-vo-lu-tions in Spain; ___ the North Pole
Wales has cop-ied my hat; with queens I've

I have char-ted, but can't get start-ed with
a-la cart-ed, but can't get start-ed with

you. ___ A-round a
you. ___ The lead-ing

golf course I'm ___ un-der par, _____ and all the
tail-ors fol-low my styles, _____ and tooth-paste

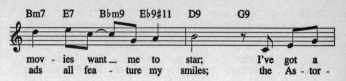

movies want me to star; I've got a
ads all fea - ture my smiles; the As - tor -

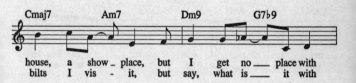

house, a show place, but I get no place with
bilts I vis - it, but say, what is it with

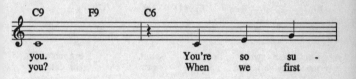

you. You're so su -
you? When we first

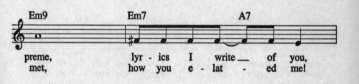

preme, lyr - ics I write of you,
met, how you e - lat - ed me!

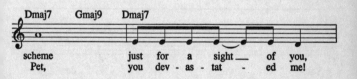

scheme just for a sight of you,
Pet, you dev - as - tat - ed me!

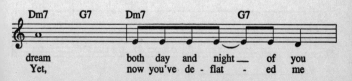

dream both day and night of you
Yet, now you've de - flat - ed me

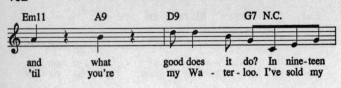

Em11 A9 D9 G7 N.C.

and what good does it do? In nine-teen
'til you're my Wa-ter-loo. I've sold my

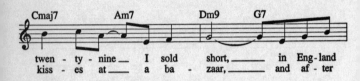

Cmaj7 Am7 Dm9 G7

twen-ty-nine___ I sold short,_____ in Eng-land
kiss-es at___ a ba-zaar,_____ and af-ter

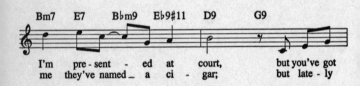

Bm7 E7 Bbm9 Eb9#11 D9 G9

I'm pre-sent - ed at court, but you've got
me they've named_ a ci - gar; but late-ly

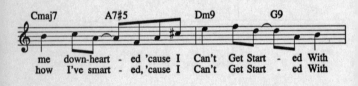

Cmaj7 A7#5 Dm9 G9

me down-heart - ed 'cause I Can't Get Start - ed With
how I've smart - ed, 'cause I Can't Get Start - ed With

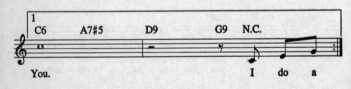

1
C6 A7#5 D9 G9 N.C.

You. I do a

2
C6 F9 C6/9

You._____

# I WISH YOU LOVE

English Words by ALBERT BEACH
French Words and Music by CHARLES TRENET

**Moderately**

I wish you blue - birds in the spring to give your heart a song to sing; and then a kiss, but more than this I Wish You Love. And in Ju - ly a lem - on - ade to cool you

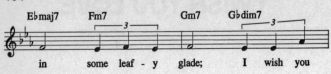

in    some    leaf - y    glade;    I    wish    you

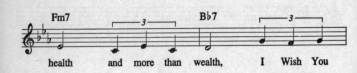

health    and    more    than    wealth,    I    Wish    You

Love. _____    My    break - ing

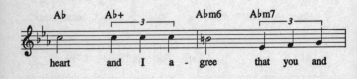

heart    and    I    a - gree    that    you    and

I    could    nev - er    be    so    with    my

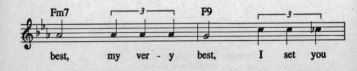

best,    my    ver - y    best,    I    set    you

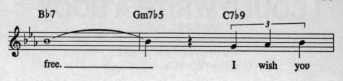

free. _____ I wish you

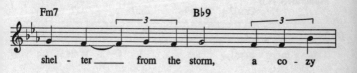

shel - ter _____ from the storm, a co - zy

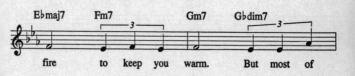

fire to keep you warm. But most of

all, when snow - flakes fall, I Wish You

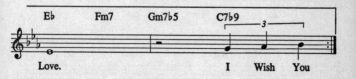

Love. I Wish You

fall, I Wish You Love. _____

# I COULD WRITE A BOOK
## from PAL JOEY

Words by LORENZ HART
Music by RICHARD RODGERS

| Dm7 | G7 | C | Am9 |

get, _____ and the sim - ple

| Dm7 | G7 | C | G7 |

se - cret of the plot _____ is just to

| C | G7 | C | C#dim7 | Dm7 |

tell them that I love you a lot, \_\_\_\_\_

| G7 | C/E | Ab7/Eb | Dm7 | G7 |

\_\_\_ then the world dis - cov - ers as

| Gm7 | C7 | F | Fm7 | Bb7 |

my book ends, how to

| C | A7 | Dm7 | G7 |

make two lov - ers of

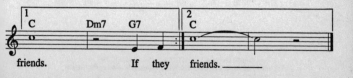

| 1. C | Dm7 | G7 | 2. C |

friends. If they friends. \_\_\_\_\_

# I LEFT MY HEART
# IN SAN FRANCISCO

Words by DOUGLAS CROSS
Music by GEORGE CORY

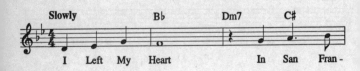

Slowly     Bb     Dm7     C#

I Left My Heart    In San Fran-

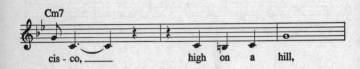

Cm7

cis-co, _____     high on a hill,

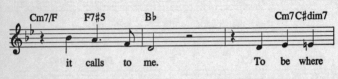

Cm7/F    F7#5    Bb       Cm7 C#dim7

it calls to me.      To be where

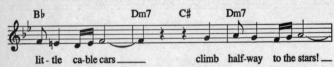

Bb     Dm7   C#   Dm7

lit-tle ca-ble cars _____    climb half-way to the stars!

D7b9    Gm7     C9     C7b9

_ The morn-ing fog _____ may chill the

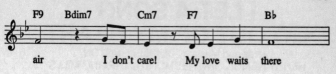

air      I don't care!    My love waits there

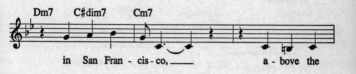

in San Fran - cis - co, _____    a - bove the

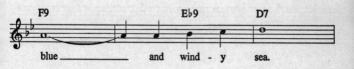

blue _____ and wind - y sea.

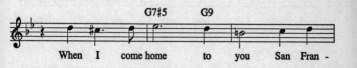

When I come home to you San Fran -

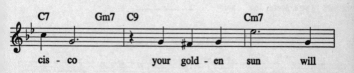

cis - co your gold - en sun will

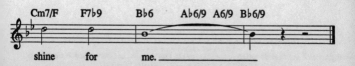

shine for me. _____

# I LET A SONG
# GO OUT OF MY HEART

Words and Music by DUKE ELLINGTON,
HENRY NEMO, JOHN REDMOND and IRVING MILLS

Moderately

I Let A Song Go Out Of My Heart,

it was the sweet-est mel - o - dy,

I know I lost heav - en 'cause

you were the song.

Since you and I have drift-ed a - part

# I WISH I WERE IN LOVE AGAIN

**from BABES IN ARMS**

Words by LORENZ HART
Music by RICHARD RODGERS

**Medium swing**

The sleep-less nights, the dai-ly fights, the
brok-en dates, the end-less waits, the

quick to-bog-gan when you reach the heights; I
love-ly lov-ing and the hate-ful hates, the

miss the kiss-es and I miss the bites, I
con-ver-sa-tion with the fly-ing plates, I

**1.** Wish I Were In Love A-gain! ___ The

**2.** Wish I Were In Love A-gain! No ___ more

# I'M BEGINNING
# TO SEE THE LIGHT

### Words and Music by DON GEORGE,
### JOHNNY HODGES, DUKE ELLINGTON and HARRY JAMES

I nev - er cared much for moon-lit skies, _ I

nev - er wink back at fi - re - flies; _ but

now that the stars are in your eyes, _ I'm Be -

gin - ning To See The Light. _ I

nev - er went in for af - ter - glow, _ or

can - dle - light on the mis - tle - toe; \_\_\_ but

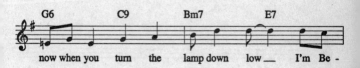

now when you turn the lamp down low \_\_ I'm Be -

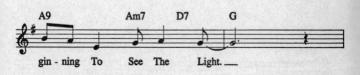

gin - ning To See The Light. \_\_

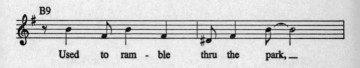

Used to ram - ble thru the park, \_\_

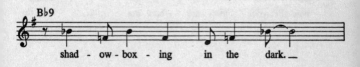

shad - ow - box - ing in the dark. \_\_

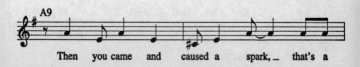

Then you came and caused a spark, \_ that's a

four - a - larm    fi - re    now. ___                    I

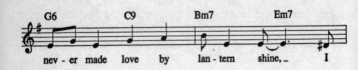

nev - er made    love    by    lan - tern    shine, ___    I

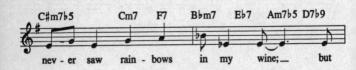

nev - er    saw    rain - bows    in my    wine; ___    but

now that your    lips    are    burn - ing    mine, ___    I'm Be -

gin-ning To    See The    Light. ___                    I    ___

# I'VE GOT YOU
# YOU UNDER MY SKIN

**from BORN TO DANCE**

### Words and Music by
### COLE PORTER

**Moderately**

I've Got You Un-der My Skin, _____ I've got you deep in the heart of me, _____ so deep in my heart, _____ you're real-ly a part of me. _____ I've Got You _____ Un-der My Skin. _____ I tried so _____

# I'M JUST A LUCKY SO AND SO

Words by MACK DAVID
Music by DUKE ELLINGTON

**Moderately**

As I walk down the street— seems ev-'ry-one I meet—
The birds in ev-'ry tree — are all so neigh-bor-ly;

gives me a friend-ly hel-lo.—} I guess I'm
They sing wher-ev-er I go.—}

just a luck-y so and so.

If you should

ask me the a-mount in my bank ac-count, I'd

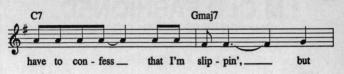

have to con - fess __ that I'm slip - pin', _____ but

that don't wor - ry me, con - fi - den - tial - ly, I've got a

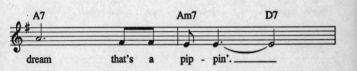

dream that's a pip - pin'. _____

And when the day is through __ each night I hur-ry to __

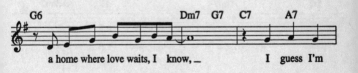

a home where love waits, I know, __ I guess I'm

just a luck - y so and so. _____

# I'M OLD FASHIONED
### from YOU WERE NEVER LOVELIER

Words by JOHNNY MERCER
Music by JEROME KERN

**Liltingly**

I'm Old Fash - ioned, I love the moon - light, I love the old fash - ioned things; _____ the sound of rain up - on a win - dow pane, the star - ry song that A - pril sings. _____ This year's

# I'VE GOT MY LOVE
# TO KEEP ME WARM

**from the 20th Century Fox Motion Picture ON THE AVENUE**

Words and Music by
IRVING BERLIN

# I'VE GOT THE WORLD
# ON A STRING

Lyric by TED KOEHLER
Music by HAROLD ARLEN

# ISN'T IT ROMANTIC?
**from the Paramount Picture LOVE ME TONIGHT**

Words by LORENZ HART
Music by RICHARD RODGERS

Isn't It Ro-man-tic? Mu-sic in the night, a dream that can be heard. Isn't It Ro-man-tic? Mov-ing shad-ows write the old-est mag-ic word. I hear the breez-es play-ing in the trees a-bove. While all the world is say-ing you were meant for love. Isn't It Ro- do you mean that I will fall in love per-chance? __ Isn't it ro-mance? ____

man-tic? Mere-ly to be young on such a night as this? Isn't It Ro-man-tic? Ev-'ry note that's sung is like a lov-er's kiss. Sweet sym-bols in the moon-light,

# IT MIGHT AS WELL BE SPRING
### from STATE FAIR

Lyrics by OSCAR HAMMERSTEIN II
Music by RICHARD RODGERS

I'm as rest-less as a wil-low in a wind-storm I'm as jump-y as a pup-pet on a string, I'd say that I had spring fev-er, but I know it is-n't spring. I am star-ry-eyed and vague-ly dis-con-tent-ed, like a night-in-gale with-out a song to

# IT COULD HAPPEN TO YOU

### from the Paramount Picture AND THE ANGELS SING

**Words by JOHNNY BURKE**
**Music by JAMES VAN HEUSEN**

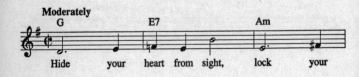

Hide your heart from sight, lock your

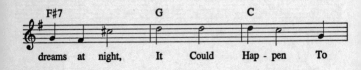

dreams at night, It Could Hap- pen To

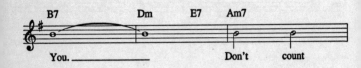

You. _____ Don't count

stars or you might stum - ble _____

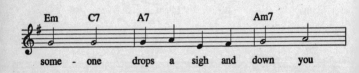

some - one drops a sigh and down you

tum - ble. Keep an eye on Spring,

run when church bells ring,

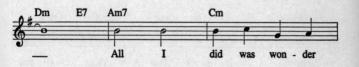

It Could Hap - pen To You.___

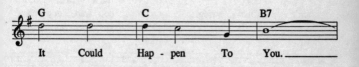

___ All I did was won - der

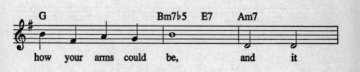

how your arms could be, and it

hap - pened to me ___

# IT DON'T MEAN A THING

### (If It Ain't Got That Swing)
### from SOPHISTICATED LADIES

**Words and Music by DUKE ELLINGTON
and IRVING MILLS**

Fm7

wah.     It     makes     no     dif - f'rence     if ___

Bb7                EbM7

___ it's     sweet     or     hot; _____     Just

Gm7                C7

give     that     rhy - thm     ev - 'ry - thing you

F7       D7              Gm     Gm/F#

got.             It     Don't     Mean     A

Gm/F    Gm/E       Eb7     D7         Gm6

Thing     if     it     ain't     got that     swing, ___

C7                     F7

doo wah, ___ doo wah,    doo wah,    doo wah,    doo wah, ___

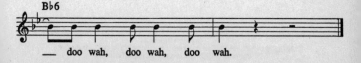

Bb6

___ doo wah,    doo wah,    doo wah.

# IT NEVER
# ENTERED MY MIND

### from HIGHER AND HIGHER

Words by LORENZ HART
Music by RICHARD RODGERS

Moderately slow

Once I laughed when I heard you say - ing

that I'd be play - ing sol - i - taire, ___

un - eas - y in my eas - y chair, ___

It Nev - er En - tered My Mind. ___

Once you told me I was mis-tak - en

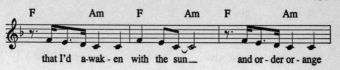

that I'd a-wak-en with the sun___ and or-der or-ange

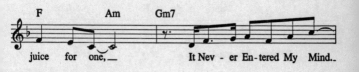

juice for one,___ It Nev-er En-tered My Mind.__

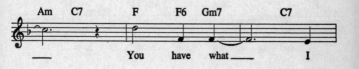

___ You have what___ I

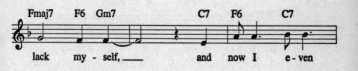

lack my-self,___ and now I e-ven

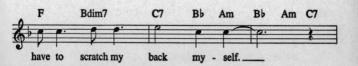

have to scratch my back my-self.___

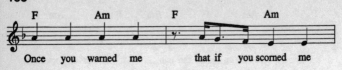

Once you warned me that if you scorned me

I'd sing the maid - en's pray'r a - gain, __

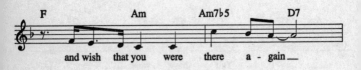

and wish that you were there a - gain __

to get in - to my hair a - gain __

It Nev - er En-tered My Mind. __

# LONG AGO
### (And Far Away)
### from COVER GIRL

### Words by IRA GERSHWIN
### Music by JEROME KERN

# JUNE IN JANUARY

**from the Paramount Picture HERE IS MY HEART**

Words and Music by LEO ROBIN
and RALPH RAINGER

Moderately

It's June In Jan - u - a - ry

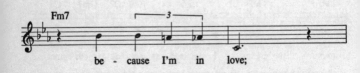

be - cause I'm in love;

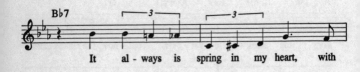

It al - ways is spring in my heart, with

you in my arms. _____ The

snow is just white blos - soms

# JUST ONE MORE CHANCE

Words by SAM COSLOW
Music by ARTHUR JOHNSTON

**Moderately slow**

Just One More Chance,__ to prove it's you a-lone I

care for, each night I say a lit-tle

prayer for Just One More Chance.__

Just one more night,__ to taste the kiss-es that en-

chant me, I'd want no oth-ers if you'd

grant me Just One More Chance.__

# THE LADY IS A TRAMP
## from BABES IN ARMS

Words by LORENZ HART
Music by RICHARD RODGERS

# THE LADY'S IN LOVE
# WITH YOU

**from the Paramount Picture SOME LIKE IT HOT**

Words by FRANK LOESSER
Music by BURTON LANE

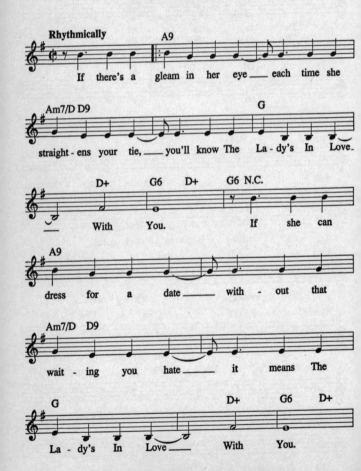

# LAZY RIVER

**Words and Music by HOAGY CARMICHAEL
and SIDNEY ARODIN**

**Moderately**

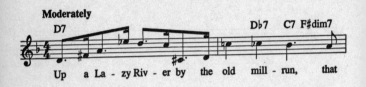

Up a La - zy Riv - er by the old mill - run, that

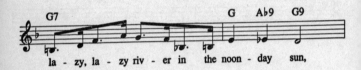

la - zy, la - zy riv - er in the noon - day sun,

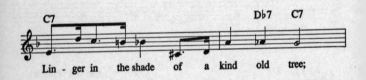

Lin - ger in the shade of a kind old tree;

throw a - way your trou - bles, dream a dream with me. —

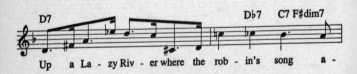

Up a La - zy Riv - er where the rob - in's song a -

wakes    a  bright    new  morn  -  ing,    we        can

loaf    a  -  long.        Blue    skies up    a- bove,

ev - 'ry-one's   in love,        up      a  La - zy Riv - er,    how

hap - py you   can be,        up    a  La - zy Riv - er    with

me.                                  me.

# LITTLE GIRL BLUE
## from JUMBO

Words by LORENZ HART
Music by RICHARD RODGERS

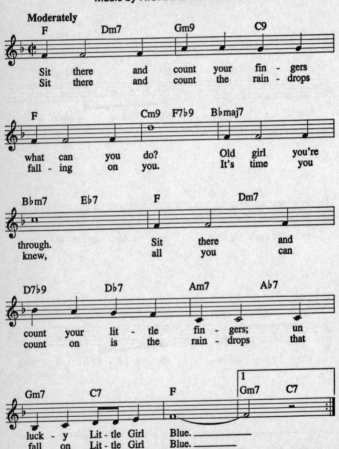

**Moderately**

F · Dm7 · Gm9 · C9

Sit there and count your fin - gers
Sit there and count the rain - drops

F · Cm9 · F7♭9 · B♭maj7

what can you do? Old girl you're
fall - ing on you. It's time you

B♭m7 · E♭7 · F · Dm7

through. Sit there and
knew, all you can

D7♭9 · D♭7 · Am7 · A♭7

count your lit - tle fin - gers; un
count on is the rain - drops that

Gm7 · C7 · F · 1. Gm7 · C7

luck - y Lit - tle Girl Blue. _____
fall on Lit - tle Girl Blue. _____

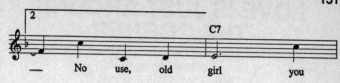

— No use, old girl you

may as well sur – ren – der, your

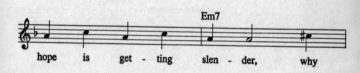

hope is get – ting slen – der, why

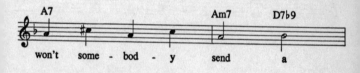

won't some – bod – y send a

ten – der blue boy to

cheer a Lit – tle Girl Blue?____

# LOVE IS JUST AROUND THE CORNER

**from the Paramount Picture HERE IS MY HEART**

Words and Music by
**LEO ROBIN and LEWIS E. GENSLER**

Love Is Just A - round The Cor - ner,
I'm a sen - ti - men - tal mourn - er,

an - y coz - y lit - tle cor - ner,
and I could - n't be for - lorn - er

Love Is Just A - round The Cor - ner when
when you keep me on a cor - ner just

I'm a - round you.
wait - ing for you.

Ve - nus de Mi - lo was

not - ed for her charms, but

strict - ly be-tween us, you're cut - er than Ve - nus and

what's more, you've got arms. So

let's go cud - dle in a cor - ner,

an - y coz - y lit - tle cor - ner.

Love Is Just A - round The Cor - ner and

I'm a - round you.

# LOVER MAN
## (Oh, Where Can You Be?)

By JIMMY DAVIS,
ROGER "RAM" RAMIREZ and JIMMY SHERMAN

**Blues tempo**

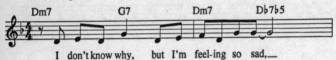

I don't know why, but I'm feel-ing so sad,___
The night is cold, and I'm so all a - lone,___
Some day we'll meet and you'll dry all my tears,___

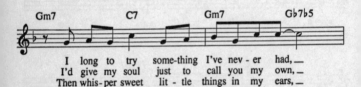

I long to try some-thing I've nev - er had, ___
I'd give my soul just to call you my own, ___
Then whis-per sweet lit - tle things in my ears, ___

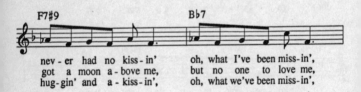

nev - er had no kiss - in' oh, what I've been miss-in',
got a moon a - bove me, but no one to love me,
hug - gin' and a - kiss - in', oh, what we've been miss-in',

**To Coda** ⊕

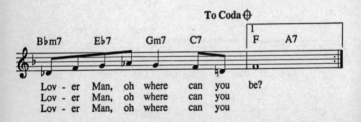

Lov - er Man, oh where can you be?
Lov - er Man, oh where can you
Lov - er Man, oh where can you

2

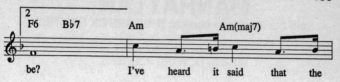

F6   Bb7    Am        Am(maj7)

be?       I've   heard   it   said    that    the

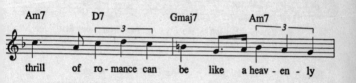

Am7     D7      Gmaj7     Am7

thrill    of   ro - mance   can    be    like   a   heav - en - ly

Bm7    Am7   D7   Gm       Gm(maj7)

dream,       I     go    to   bed    with     a

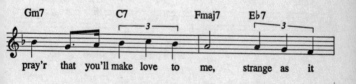

Gm7      C7       Fmaj7     Eb7

pray'r   that   you'll   make   love   to    me,     strange   as   it

**D.C. al Coda**

Em7b5    A7

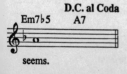

seems.

**CODA**

F6

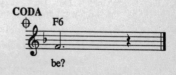

be?

# MANHATTAN
### from the Broadway Musical THE GARRICK GAIETIES

Words by LORENZ HART
Music by RICHARD RODGERS

We'll have Man-hat-tan the Bronx and Stat-en
We'll go to Green-wich where mod-ern men itch

Is-land too; \_\_\_\_\_ it's love-ly
to be free; \_\_\_\_\_ and Bowl-ing

go-ing through \_\_\_\_\_ the Zoo. \_\_\_\_\_
Green you'll see \_\_\_\_\_ with me. \_\_\_\_\_

It's ver-y fan-cy
We'll bathe at Bright-on,

on old De-lan-cey Street, you know; \_\_\_\_\_
the fish you'll fright-en when you're in \_\_\_\_\_

— the sub - way charms us so, _____
— your bath - ing suit so thin _____

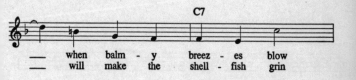

— when balm - y breez - es blow
— will make the shell - fish grin

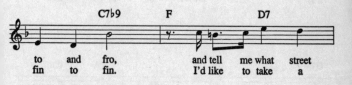

to and fro, and tell me what street
fin to fin. I'd like to take a

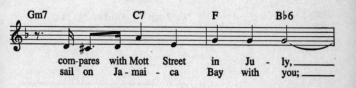

com - pares with Mott Street in Ju - ly, _____
sail on Ja - mai - ca Bay with you; _____

— sweet push carts gen - tly glid -
— and fair Can - ar - sie's Lakes _____

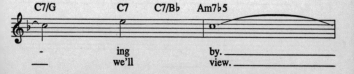

- ing by. _____
— we'll view. _____

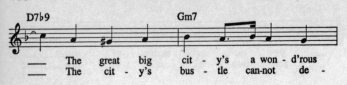

The great big cit - y's a won - d'rous
The cit - y's bus - tle can-not de -

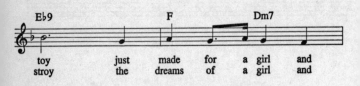

toy just made for a girl and
stroy the dreams of a girl and

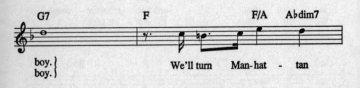

boy.
boy. We'll turn Man-hat - tan

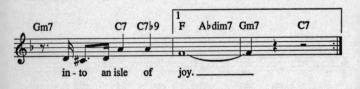

in - to an isle of joy. _____

joy. _____

# MAS QUE NADA

Words and Music by
JORGE BEN

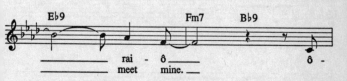

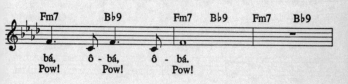

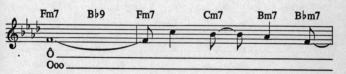

160

ô - bá, ô - bá, ô - bá.
Ow! Ow! Ow!

Mas Que Na - da sai da mi - nha
It's a feel - ing that be - gins to

fren - te que eu que - ro pas - sar, pois o
grow an' grow an' grow in - side me 'til I

sam - ba es - tá a - ni - ma - do. O que
feel like I'm gon - na ex - plode. Oh, this is

eu que - ro é sam - bar,
what you do to me.

Es - se sam - ba que é mix -
Are your lips say - ing things

- to de ma - ra ca - tú,
that you feel in your heart?

é sam - ba de pre - to ve - lho,
If your heart is beat - ing mad - ly,

161

# MEDITATION
## (MEDITACÁO)

Music by ANTONIO CARLOS JOBIM
English Words by NORMAN GIMBEL

Medium bossa nova

In _____ my lone-
Though _____ you're far _____
I _____ will wait _____

- li - ness _____ when you're gone
— a - way _____ I have on -
— for you _____ 'til the sun

— and I'm all ___ by my - self ___ and I ___ need your___
- ly to close ___ my eyes ___ and you ___ are back___
— falls from out ___ of the sky ___ for what ___ else can

— ca - ress.
— to stay.
— I do? _____

I _____ just think ___
I _____ just close ___
I _____ will wait ___

# MISTY

Words by JOHNNY BURKE
Music by ERROLL GARNER

Slowly, with a smooth swing

Look at me,
I'm as
way own,
and as a
would I

help-less as a kit-ten up a
thou-sand vi-o-lins be-gin to
wan-der through this won-der-land a-

tree and I feel like I'm cling-ing to a cloud, I
play, or it might be the sound of your hel-lo, that
lone, nev-er know-ing my right foot from my left, my

can't__ un-der-stand,__ I get Mist-y just hold-ing your
mu-sic I hear,__ I get Mist-y the mo-ment you're
hat__ from my glove,__ I'm too Mist-y and too much in

hand.__ Walk my

near.

You can say that you're

lead-ing me on, _____ but it's just what I

want you to do. __ Don't you no-tice how

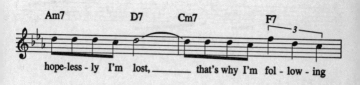

hope-less-ly I'm lost, _____ that's why I'm fol-low-ing

you. _____ On my

**CODA**

love. _____

# MONA LISA

**from the Paramount Picture CAPTAIN CAREY, U.S.A.**

Words and Music by
JAY LIVINGSTON and RAY EVANS

Mo - na Li - sa, Mo - na Li - sa men have

named you; You're so like the la - dy with the mys - tic

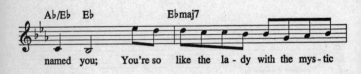

smile. Is it on - ly 'cause you're lone - ly ___ they have

blamed you for that Mo - na Li - sa strange-ness ___ in your

smile? Do you smile to tempt a lov - er, ___ Mo - na

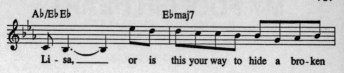

Li - sa, _____ or is this your way to hide a bro-ken

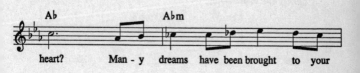

heart? Man - y dreams have been brought to your

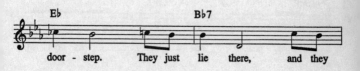

door - step. They just lie there, and they

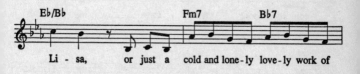

die there. Are you warm, are you real, Mo - na

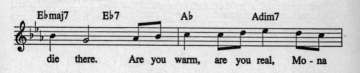

Li - sa, or just a cold and lone-ly love-ly work of

art?       Mo - na art?

# MY FOOLISH HEART

### from MY FOOLISH HEART

**Words by NED WASHINGTON**
**Music by VICTOR YOUNG**

Slowly and expressively

The night _____ is like a

love - ly tune, be - ware _____ My Fool - ish

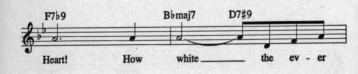

Heart! How white _____ the ev - er

con - stant moon; take care _____ My Fool - ish

Heart! There's a line be - tween love and fas - ci -

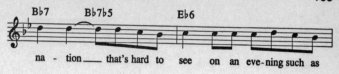

na - tion___ that's hard to see on an eve-ning such as

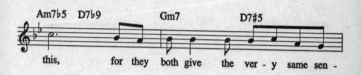

this, for they both give the ver - y same sen -

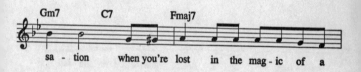

sa - tion when you're lost in the mag - ic of a

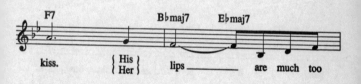

kiss. { His } { Her } lips ___ are much too

close to mine, be - ware ___ My Fool - ish

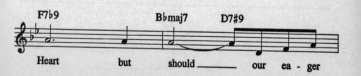

Heart but should ___ our ea - ger

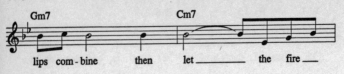

lips com - bine      then      let ____ the fire ____

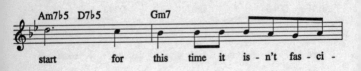

start      for      this      time it      is - n't      fas - ci -

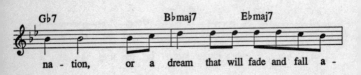

na - tion,      or      a      dream      that will fade and fall      a -

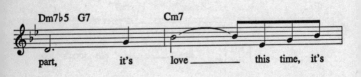

part,      it's      love ____      this      time,      it's

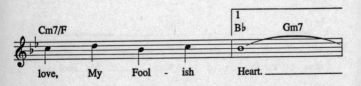

love,      My      Fool - ish      Heart. ____

____      The      Heart. ____

# ONE NOTE SAMBA
## (Samba De Uma Nota So)

Original Words by NEWTON MENDONCA
English Words by ANTONIO CARLOS JOBIM
Music by ANTONIO CARLOS JOBIM

**Samba**

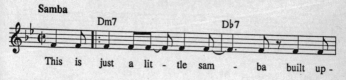

This is just a lit - tle sam - ba built up-

on a sin - gle note. ___ Oth - er

notes are bound ___ to fol - low but the

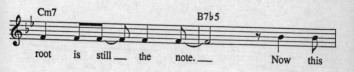

root is still ___ the note. ___ Now this

new one is ___ the con - se - quence ___ of the

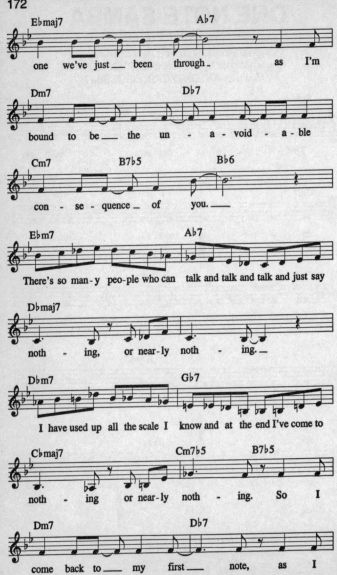

# MY FUNNY VALENTINE

### from BABES IN ARMS

Words by LORENZ HART
Music by RICHARD RODGERS

**Slowly**

My Fun - ny Val - en-tine, sweet com - ic

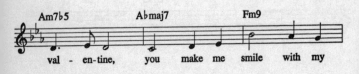

val - en-tine, you make me smile with my

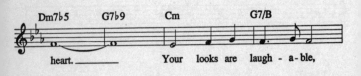

heart. _____ Your looks are laugh - a - ble,

un - pho - to - graph - a - ble, yet, you're my

fav - 'rite work of art. _____ Is your

# NATURE BOY

Words and Music by
EDEN AHBEZ

# NEVER LET ME GO
## from the Paramount Picture THE SCARLET HOUR

**Words and Music by JAY LIVINGSTON
and RAY EVANS**

# A NIGHTINGALE SANG IN BERKELEY SQUARE

Lyric by ERIC MASCHWITZ
Music by MANNING SHERWIN

Night-in-gale Sang In Berk - 'ley Square.

The moon that lin-gered o-ver Lon-don town,_ poor
When dawn came steal-ing up all gold and blue _ to

puz-zled moon, he wore a frown, how could he know we two were
in-ter-rupt our ren-dez-vous, I still re-mem-ber how you

so in love?_ The whole damn world seemed up-side down the
smiled and said _ "Was that a dream or was it true?" Our

streets of town were paved with stars. It was such a ro-man-tic af-
home-ward step was just as light as the tap-danc-ing feet of As-

fair and as we kiss'd and said "good-night"
taire. And like an e-cho far a-way

Night-in-gale Sang In Berk - 'ley Square. ___ How

Square. I know 'cause I was there

that night in Berk - 'ley Square. ___

# OLD DEVIL MOON
## from FINIAN'S RAINBOW

Words by E.Y. HARBURG
Music by BURTON LANE

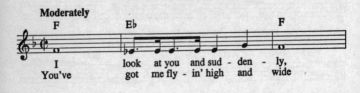

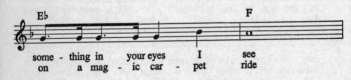

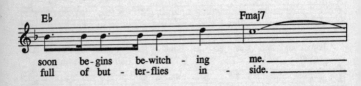

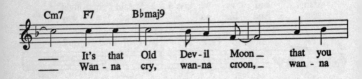

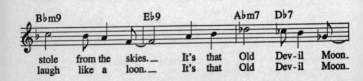

# OUT OF NOWHERE
## from the Paramount Picture DUDE RANCH

Words by EDWARD HEYMAN
Music by JOHNNY GREEN

You came to me _____ from Out Of No - where, _____ you took my heart _____ and found it free. _____ Won - der - ful dreams, _____ won - der - ful schemes ___ from no - where made ev - 'ry hour

# PERFIDIA

### Words and Music by
### ALBERTO DOMINGUEZ

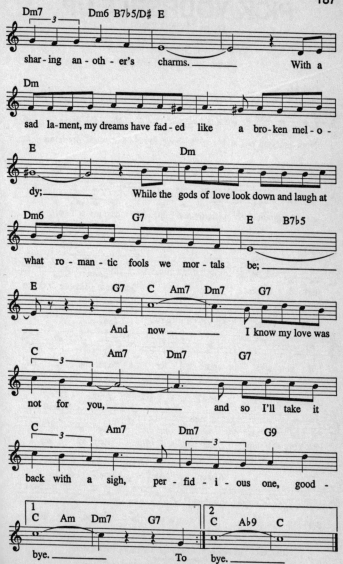

# PICK YOURSELF UP
### from SWING TIME

Words by DOROTHY FIELDS
Music by JEROME KERN

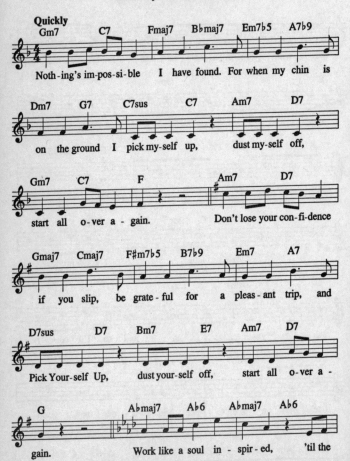

# PRELUDE TO A KISS

**Words by IRVING GORDON and IRVING MILLS**
**Music by DUKE ELLINGTON**

# QUIET NIGHTS OF QUIET STARS

English Words by GENE LEES
Original Words and Music by ANTONIO CARLOS JOBIM

to be. — Here, with you so close—

to me — un - til — the fi - nal

flick-er of — life's em - ber. _____

I, who— was lost and lone - ly,— be-liev-ing life was

on - ly— a bit-ter tra-gic joke, have found—with you,—

_____ the mean-ing of ex -

ist-ence. Oh,— my love. _____

# ROUTE 66

### By BOBBY TROUP

**Moderately**

If you ____ ev-er plan to mo-tor west,__ __ Trav-el my way, take the high-way that's the best. __ Get your kicks on Route __ Six-ty-six! It winds ____ from Chi-ca-go to L. A., __ more than two ____ thou-sand miles all the way. __

# SOLITUDE

Words and Music by DUKE ELLINGTON,
EDDIE DE LANGE and IRVING MILLS

In my Sol - i - tude _____ you
Sol - i - tude _____ you
Sol - i - tude _____ I'm

haunt me with re - ver - ies _____
taunt me with mem - o - ries _____
pray - ing, dear Lord a - bove _____

_____ of days gone by. _____ In my
_____ that nev - er
_____ send back my

die. _____ I sit in my chair, I'm

filled with de - spair, there's no one could be so sad. _____ With

gloom ev - 'ry - where, I sit and I stare, I know that I'll soon go

mad. In my

love. _____

# SMOKE GETS IN YOUR EYES

**from ROBERTA**

Words by OTTO HARBACH
Music by JEROME KERN

They asked me how I knew my true love was true? ___

___ I of course re - plied, "Some-thing here in -

side, can - not be de - nied."___

They said some-day you'll find, all who love are blind.___

___ When your heart's on fire, you must re - al -

ize Smoke Gets In Your Eyes.___

# THE SONG IS YOU

## from MUSIC IN THE AIR

Lyrics by OSCAR HAMMERSTEIN II
Music by JEROME KERN

I hear mu-sic when I look at you; _____ a beau-ti-ful theme of ev-'ry dream I ev-er knew. _____ Down deep in my heart _____ I hear it play. _____ I feel it start, _____ then melt a-way. I hear mu-sic when I touch your hand; _____ a beau-ti-ful mel-o-dy from some en-chant-ed land. _____ Down deep in my heart, _____ I hear it say, _____ is this the day?

# STELLA BY STARLIGHT

**from the Paramount Picture THE UNINVITED**

Words by NED WASHINGTON
Music by VICTOR YOUNG

# TAKE THE "A" TRAIN

Words and Music by
BILLY STRAYHORN

**Easy Swing**

C6        D7♭5

You _____ must take the "A" Train _____
If _____ you miss the "A" Train,

Dm7     G7            C

To     go to Sug-ar Hill way up in Har-lem. _____
You'll   find you've missed the quick-est way to Har-lem. _____

Fmaj7

Hur-ry, _____ get on now it's

D7

com-ing. _____ Lis-ten to those rails a-

Dm9   G9       D♭9   C6

thrum-ming. _____ All 'board! _____ Get on the

D7♭5                Dm7

"A" Train, _____ soon

G7              C

you will be on Sug-ar Hill in Har-lem.

# STEPPIN' OUT
# WITH MY BABY
### from the Motion Picture Irving Berlin's EASTER PARADE

Words and Music by
**IRVING BERLIN**

206

# A SUNDAY KIND OF LOVE

**Words and Music by BARBARA BELLE, LOUIS PRIMA,
ANITA LEONARD and STAN RHODES**

I want A Sun-day Kind Of Love,
love that's on the square,
some-one to en-fold

a love to last past Sat-ur-day night.
can't seem to find some-bod-y to care.
to keep me warm when Mon-days are cold.

I'd like to know it's more than love at first sight.
I'm on a lone-ly road that leads me no-where.
A love for all my life to have and to hold.

To Coda

I want A Sun-day Kind Of Love,
I need A Sun-day Kind Of Love,
I want A Sun-day Kind Of Love.

I want a I

# SWAY
## (QUIEN SERA)

English Words by NORMAN GIMBEL
Spanish Words and Music by PABLO BELTRAN RUIZ

**Moderately**

F#dim7  B7  F#dim7 B7

When ma-rim-ba rhy-thms start to play, dance with me,
*Quien se-rá la que me quie-ra a mi* *Quien se-rá*

Em

make me sway.\_ Like the la-zy o-cean
*Quien se - rá* *Quien se - rá la que me*

C9#11 C9 B9   C9#11 C9 B7b9   Em6 B7b9 Em6

hugs the shore, hold me close, sway me more.
*dé su a-mor* *Quien se - rá* *Quien se - rá*

F#dim7  B7  F#dim7  B7

\_ Like a flow-er bend-ing in the breeze, bend with me,
*Yo no sé si la po-dré en-con-trar* *yo no sé*

Em

sway with ease.\_ When we dance you have a
*yo no sé\_* *Yo no sé si vol-ve-*

C9#11 C9 B9   C9#11 C9 B7b9   Em6 B7b9 Em6

way with me, stay with me, sway with me.\_
*ré a que-rer* *Yo no sé* *Yo no sé\_\_\_*

G6/B Bbdim7   D7/A   D7

\_ Oth-er dan-cers may be on the floor, dear, but my eyes will
*He que-ri-do vol-ver a vi-vir* *La pa-sión y el ca-*

**G**

see on - ly you._____ On - ly you have that
lor de o-tro a - mor _____ de o tro a-mor que me hi -

**B7**                      **Em**     **C9 B7b9**

mag - ic tech-nique,___ when we sway I grow weak.
cie - ra sen-tir___ que me hi-cie - ra fe - liz co-mo a-yer lo

**Em**            **F#dim7**   **B7**    **F#dim7**   **B7**

I can hear the sound of vi - o-lins, long be-fore
fui quien se - rá la que me quie-ra a mí Quien se - rá

**Em**                     **C9#11 C9 B9**

it be-gins.___ Make me thrill as on - ly you know how,
Quien se - rá___ Quien se - rá la que me dé su a-mor

**C9#11**    **C9**   **B7b9**     **1** **Em6**   **B7b9 Em6**

sway me smooth, sway me now.___
Quien se - rá Quien se - rá

**2** **Em6**   **B7b9**    **Em6**

When ma - rim - ba rhy-thms sway me now.___
Quien se - rá la que me Quien se - rá___

**B7**                   **Em**

Sway me smooth, sway me now._____
Quien se - rá, quien se - rá._____

# TAIN'T NOBODY'S BIZ-NESS IF I DO

**Words and Music by PORTER GRAINGER
and EVERETT ROBBINS**

**Moderate Blues tempo**

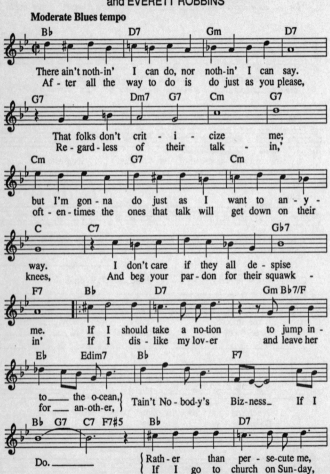

There ain't noth-in' I can do, nor noth-in' I can say,
Af-ter all the way to do is do just as you please,

That folks don't crit-i-cize me;
Re-gard-less of their talk-in,'

but I'm gon-na do just as I want to an-y-
oft-en-times the ones that talk will get down on their

way. I don't care if they all de-spise
knees, And beg your par-don for their squawk-

me.' If I should take a no-tion to jump in
in' If I dis-like my lov-er and leave her

to __ the o-cean,}
for __ an-oth-er,} Tain't No-bod-y's Biz-ness__ If I

Do. ____ {Rath-er than per-se-cute me,
{If I go to church on Sun-day,

# THAT OLD BLACK MAGIC

### from the Paramount Picture STAR SPANGLED RHYTHM

Words by JOHNNY MERCER
Music by HAROLD ARLEN

**Easy Swing**

That Old Black Mag - ic has me in its spell. That Old Black Mag - ic that you weave so well. Those i - cy fin - gers up and down my spine. The same old witch- craft when your eyes meet mine. The

# THERE'S A SMALL HOTEL

## from ON YOUR TOES

Words by LORENZ HART
Music by RICHARD RODGERS

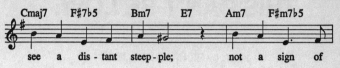

see a dis-tant steep-ple; not a sign of

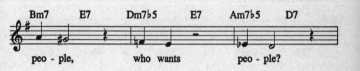

peo-ple, who wants peo-ple?

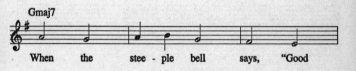

When the stee-ple bell says, "Good

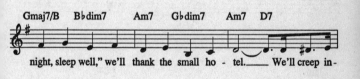

night, sleep well," we'll thank the small ho-tel.____ We'll creep in-

to our lit-tle shell____ and we will thank the small ho-

tel to-geth-er. _____

# THIS CAN'T BE LOVE
## from THE BOYS FROM SYRACUSE

### Words by LORENZ HART
### Music by RICHARD RODGERS

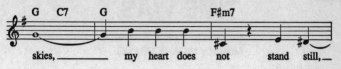

skies, _____ my heart does not stand still, \_

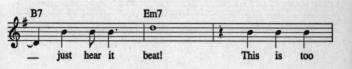

\_ just hear it beat! This is too

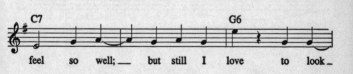

sweet to be

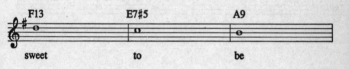

love. This Can't Be Love be - cause I

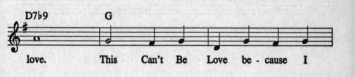

feel so well; \_ but still I love to look \_

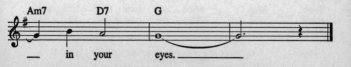

\_ in your eyes. \_\_\_\_\_

# TIME WAS

English Words by S.K. RUSSELL
Music by MIGUEL PRADO

**Moderately**

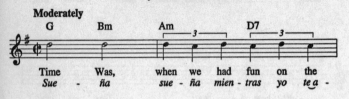

Time    Was,    when we had fun on the
*Sue  -  ña    sue - ña mien - tras yo te a -*

school - yard swings,    when we ex - changed grad - u -
*rru - lla - ré    con el he - chi - zo de és -*

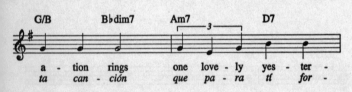

a  -  tion rings    one love - ly yes - ter -
*ta can - ción    que pa - ra tí for -*

day. _____
*jé. _____*

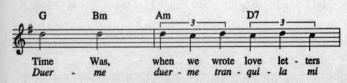

Time    Was,    when we wrote love let - ters
*Duer  -  me    duer - me tran - qui - la mi*

223

which I've a place in your heart.
*tú      mu - jer - ci - ta      i - deal.*

Dar  -  ling,      ev - 'ry to - mor - row will
*Duer  -  me      duer - me mien - tras yo te a -*

be  com - plete,      if all our mo - ments are
*rru  -  lla - ré      con el he - chi - zo de és -*

half  as  sweet      as all our Time Was
*ta o - ra - ción      que pa - ra tí can -*

1.
then. _____
*té. _____*

2.
then. _____
*té. _____*

# THE WAY YOU LOOK TONIGHT

## from SWING TIME

Words by DOROTHY FIELDS
Music by JEROME KERN

# TO EACH HIS OWN
### from the Paramount Picture TO EACH HIS OWN

**Words and Music by JAY LIVINGSTON
and RAY EVANS**

A
rose \_\_\_\_ must re-main \_\_\_\_ with the
good \_\_\_\_ is a song \_\_\_\_ if the

sun \_\_\_\_ and the rain \_\_\_\_ or its love-ly prom-ise won't come
words just don't be-long \_\_\_\_ and a dream must be a dream for

true. \_\_\_\_ To Each His Own, To
two. \_\_\_\_ No good a-lone, To

Each His Own,
Each His Own, and my own is

you. \_\_\_\_ What for me there's

you. \_\_\_\_ If a flame is to grow there

# THE VERY THOUGHT
# OF YOU

### Words and Music by
### RAY NOBLE

The Ve - ry Thought Of You, _____ and I for -
get to do _____ the lit - tle
or - din - ar - y things that ev - 'ry one
ought to do. _____ I'm liv - ing
in a kind of day - dream, I'm
hap - py as a king, and
fool - ish tho' it may seem, to

# WATCH WHAT HAPPENS

## from THE UMBRELLAS OF CHERBOURG

Music by MICHEL LEGRAND
Original French Text by JACQUES DEMY
English Lyrics by NORMAN GIMBEL

# WHAT A WONDERFUL WORLD

**featured in the Motion Picture GOOD MORNING VIETNAM**

**Words and Music by GEORGE DAVID WEISS
and BOB THIELE**

# WHAT IS THERE TO SAY?

## from THE ZIEGFELD FOLLIES OF 1934

### Words and Music by VERNON DUKE
### and E.Y. HARBURG

Slowly

What Is There To Say and

what is there to do? The

dream I've been seek-ing has, prac-ti-c'lly speak-ing, come

true. What Is There To

Say and how will I pull

through? I knew in a mo-ment, con-

# WHAT'LL I DO?
## from MUSIC BOX REVUE OF 1924

Words and Music by
IRVING BERLIN

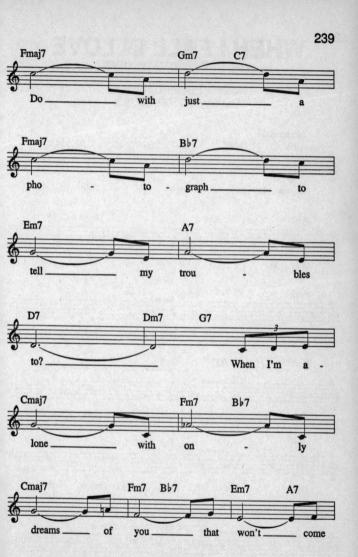

# WHEN I FALL IN LOVE
## from ONE MINUTE TO ZERO

Words by EDWARD HEYMAN
Music by VICTOR YOUNG

Eb     C7b9#5     Fm7    Bb7   Eb     C7b9#5

When I give my heart     it will be com -

Fm7     Bb7     Eb         Db9     C9#5

plete - ly     or I'll nev - er give     my

Fm7      Bb7         Eb

heart. _____     And the mo - ment I can

Ab         Gm7    C7     Fm7   Db9

feel that you feel that way too,     is

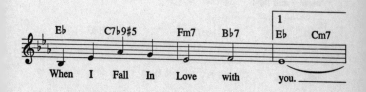

Eb     C7b9#5     Fm7    Bb7     **1** Eb    Cm7

When I Fall In Love with you. _____

Fm7     Bb7b9     **2** Eb

_____     you. _____

# WHEN SUNNY GETS BLUE

Lyric by JACK SEGAL
Music by MARVIN FISHER

**Slow Blues tempo**

When Sun - ny Gets Blue, her eyes get gray and cloud-y.
Sun - ny Gets Blue, she breathes a sigh of sad-ness,

Then the rain be - gins to fall.
like the wind that stirs the trees.

Pit - ter pat - ter, pit - ter pat - ter, love is gone so what can mat-ter?
Wind that sets the leaves to sway-in', like some vi - o - lins are play-in'

No sweet lov - er man comes to call. _____ When
weird and hant - ing mel - o -

dies. Peo - ple used to love to

hear her laugh, see her smile. That's how she got her

# WHERE OR WHEN
## from BABES IN ARMS

Words by LORENZ HART
Music by RICHARD RODGERS

Moderately

It seems we stood and talked like this be-fore. We looked at each oth-er in the same way then, but I can't re-mem-ber When Or When. The clothes you're wear-ing are the clothes you wore. The smile you are smil-ing you were smil-ing then, but I can't re-mem-ber Where Or When.

# YOU TOOK ADVANTAGE OF ME

## from PRESENT ARMS

Words by LORENZ HART
Music by RICHARD RODGERS

Moderately

I'm a sen-ti-men-tal sap, that's all. What's the use of try-ing not to fall? I have no will, you've made your kill 'cause You Took Ad-van-tage Of Me! I'm just like an ap-ple on a bough, and you're gon-na shake me down some-how, so what's the use? You've cooked my goose 'cause You Took Ad-van-tage Of

# YOU'D BE SO NICE
# TO COME HOME TO

**from SOMETHING TO SHOUT ABOUT**

Words and Music by
COLE PORTER

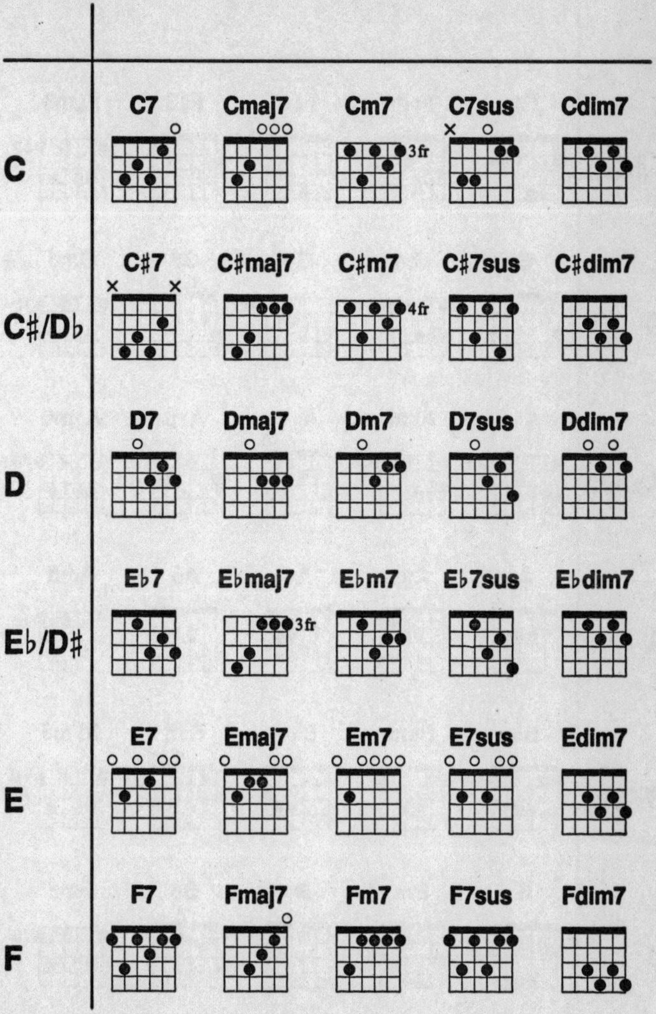

**C**

| C7 | Cmaj7 | Cm7 | C7sus | Cdim7 |

**C#/Db**

| C#7 | C#maj7 | C#m7 | C#7sus | C#dim7 |

**D**

| D7 | Dmaj7 | Dm7 | D7sus | Ddim7 |

**Eb/D#**

| Eb7 | Ebmaj7 | Ebm7 | Eb7sus | Ebdim7 |

**E**

| E7 | Emaj7 | Em7 | E7sus | Edim7 |

**F**

| F7 | Fmaj7 | Fm7 | F7sus | Fdim7 |

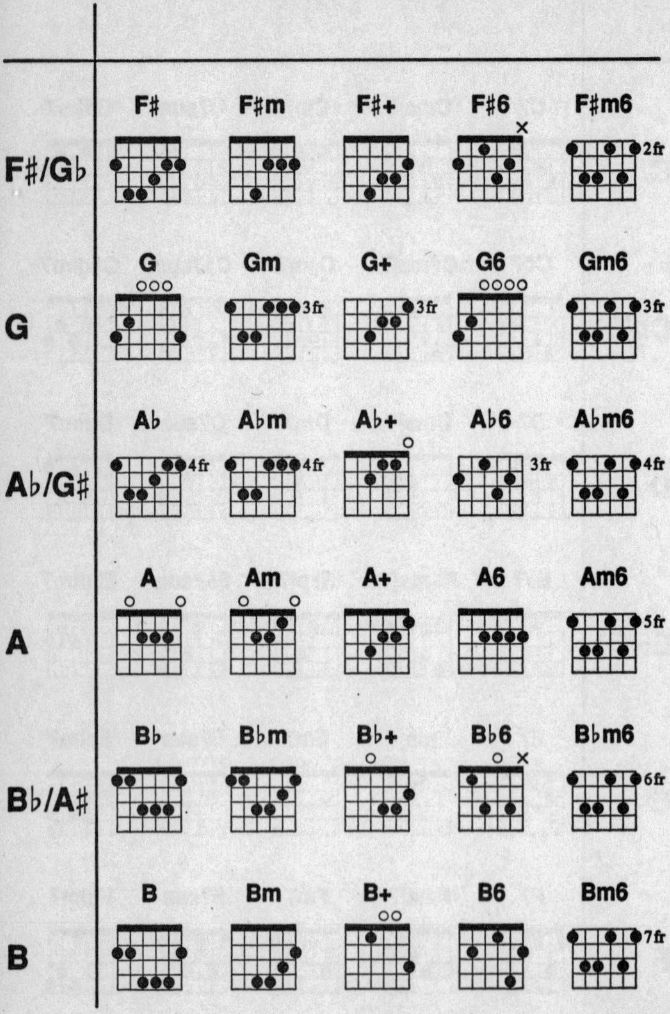
F#/Gb
F# F#m F#+ F#6 F#m6
2fr
G
G Gm Gm+ G6 Gm6
3fr 3fr 3fr
Ab/G#
Ab Abm Ab+ Ab6 Abm6
4fr 4fr 3fr 4fr
A
A Am A+ A6 Am6
5fr
Bb/A#
Bb Bbm Bb+ Bb6 Bbm6
6fr
B
B Bm B+ B6 Bm6
7fr

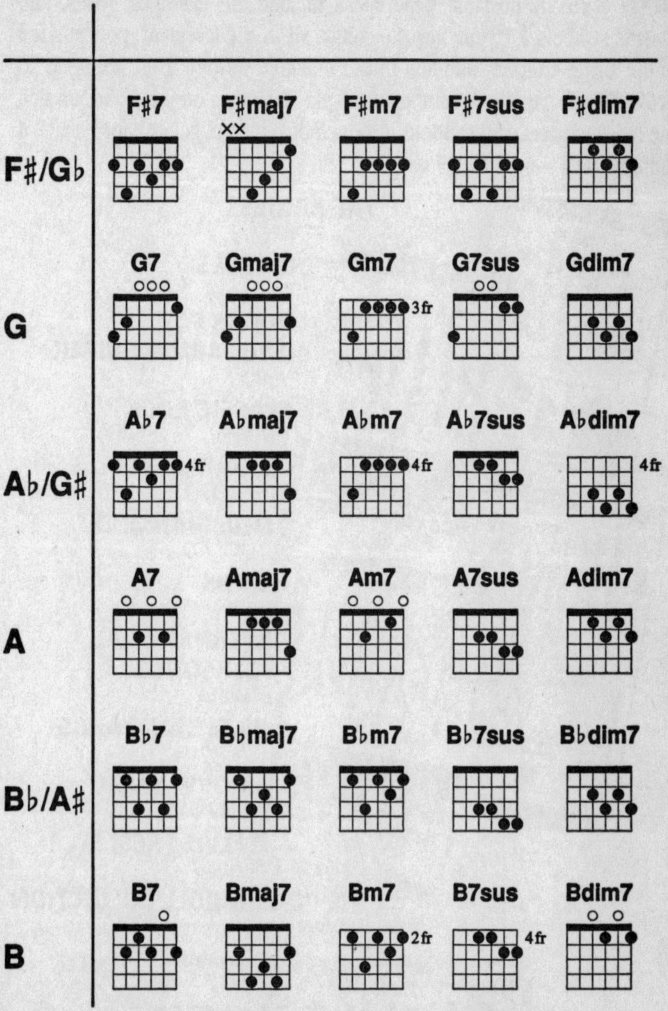

This page is a guitar chord chart showing chord diagrams organized by root note and chord type.

| | F#7 | F#maj7 | F#m7 | F#7sus | F#dim7 |
|---|---|---|---|---|---|
| **F#/Gb** | | ×× | | | |

| | G7 | Gmaj7 | Gm7 | G7sus | Gdim7 |
|---|---|---|---|---|---|
| **G** | ○○○ | ○○○ | 3fr | ○○ | |

| | Ab7 | Abmaj7 | Abm7 | Ab7sus | Abdim7 |
|---|---|---|---|---|---|
| **Ab/G#** | 4fr | | 4fr | | 4fr |

| | A7 | Amaj7 | Am7 | A7sus | Adim7 |
|---|---|---|---|---|---|
| **A** | ○ ○ ○ | | ○ ○ ○ | | |

| | Bb7 | Bbmaj7 | Bbm7 | Bb7sus | Bbdim7 |
|---|---|---|---|---|---|
| **Bb/A#** | | | | | |

| | B7 | Bmaj7 | Bm7 | B7sus | Bdim7 |
|---|---|---|---|---|---|
| **B** | ○ | | 2fr | 4fr | ○ ○ |

These perfectly portable paperbacks include the melodies, lyrics, and chords symbols for your favorite songs, all in a convenient, pocket-sized book. Using concise, one-line music notation, anyone from hobbyists to professionals can strum on the guitar, play melodies on the piano, or sing the lyrics to great songs. Books also include a helpful guitar chord chart. A fantastic deal – **only $5.95 each!**

### THE BEATLES
00702008

### THE BLUES
00702014

### CHORDS FOR KEYBOARD & GUITAR
00702009

### CLASSIC ROCK
00310058

### COUNTRY HITS
00702013

### NEIL DIAMOND
00702012

### HYMNS
00240103

### INTERNATIONAL FOLKSONGS
00240104

### JAZZ STANDARDS
00240114

### MOVIE MUSIC
00240113

### ELVIS PRESLEY
00240102

### THE ROCK & ROLL COLLECTION
00702020

FOR MORE INFORMATION, SEE YOUR LOCAL MUSIC DEALER,
OR WRITE TO:

**HAL•LEONARD™**
**C O R P O R A T I O N**
7777 W. BLUEMOUND RD. P.O. BOX 13819 MILWAUKEE, WI 53213